This Book
Belongs to

....

Deidra Acosta

Hi, Im Deidra Acosta and these are 4 of my horses. The grey mare was purchased from an auction and was likely headed to slaughter due to having a bad front leg. I was not letting that happen to her especially only being 6 years old. Once home it was apparent she had been abused and was scared to death to be tied up for anything and also feared men, I cant even tell you her registered name, I call her Freckles. She had her 1st filly whom is the big sorrel in the front with her colt. The sorrel was the first baby that was born on the farm with me and I raised from birth. Her name is girlfriend and she is a grand daughter of Seattle Slew on her sires side. Both babies in this photo are colts, the black one laying down behind his mother the grey mare is hungry Harry, since he had he nose in the grain almost from day 1. The bay colt standing by his mom Girlfriend is affectionately called lil shit...he was an onery lil fellow plus got the scours at 3 days old. This photo shows 3 generations of horses. It was hard to choose which photo to submit since I had 10 other gorgeous horses. All of them have been an important part of my life and got me thru some really rough times with their loyalty, kindness and companionship. I dont know how I would live without all my fantastic 4 legged friends!

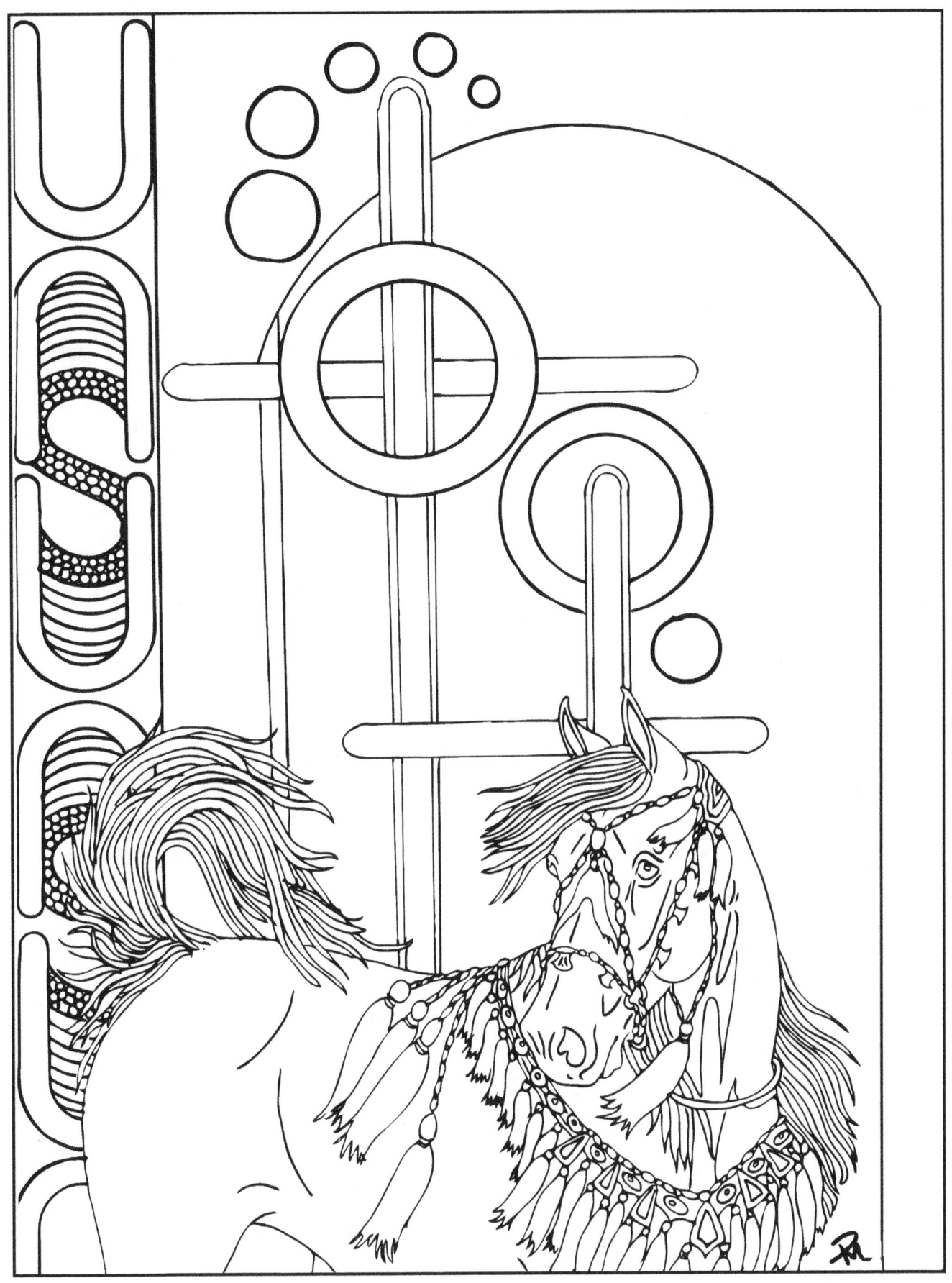

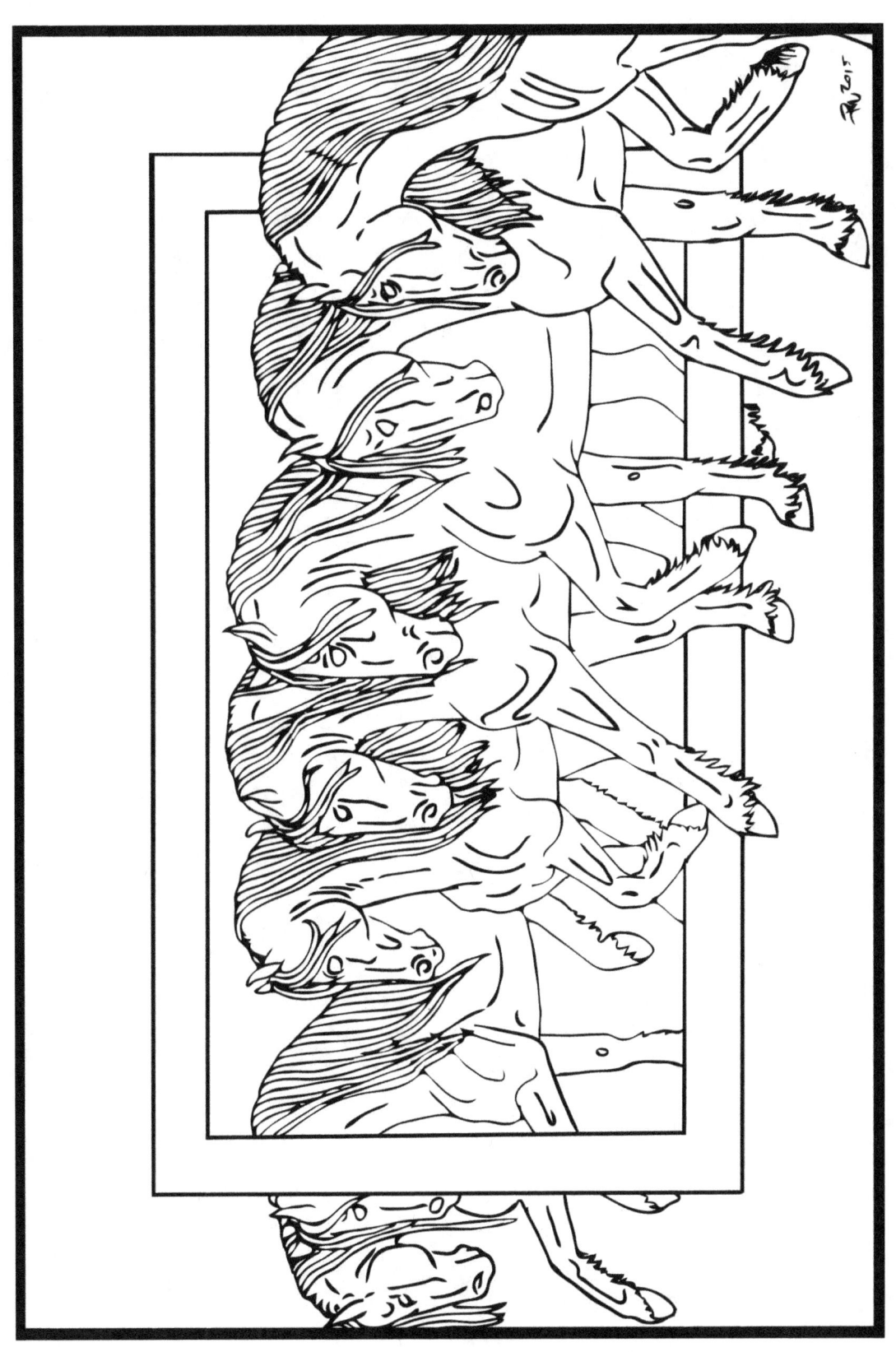

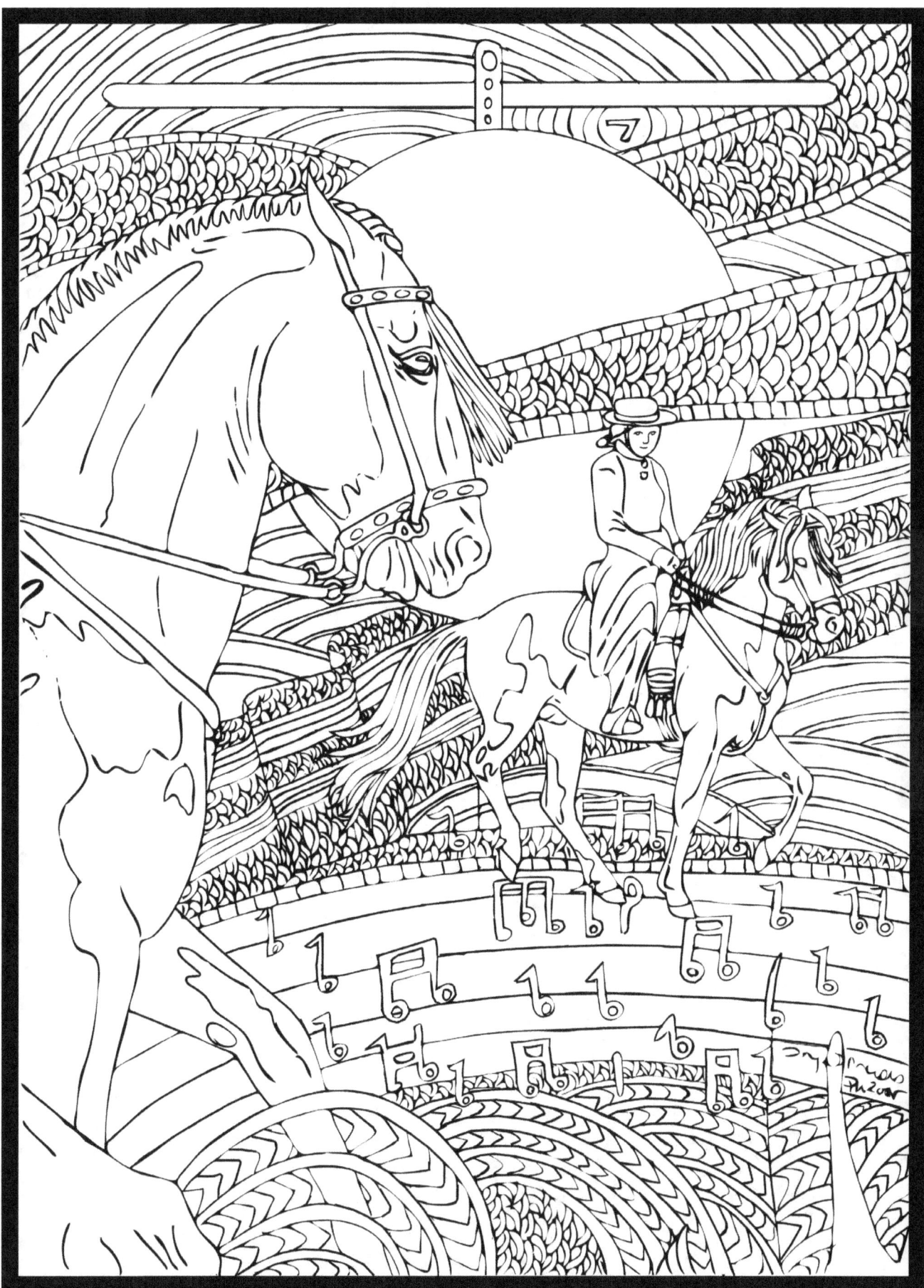

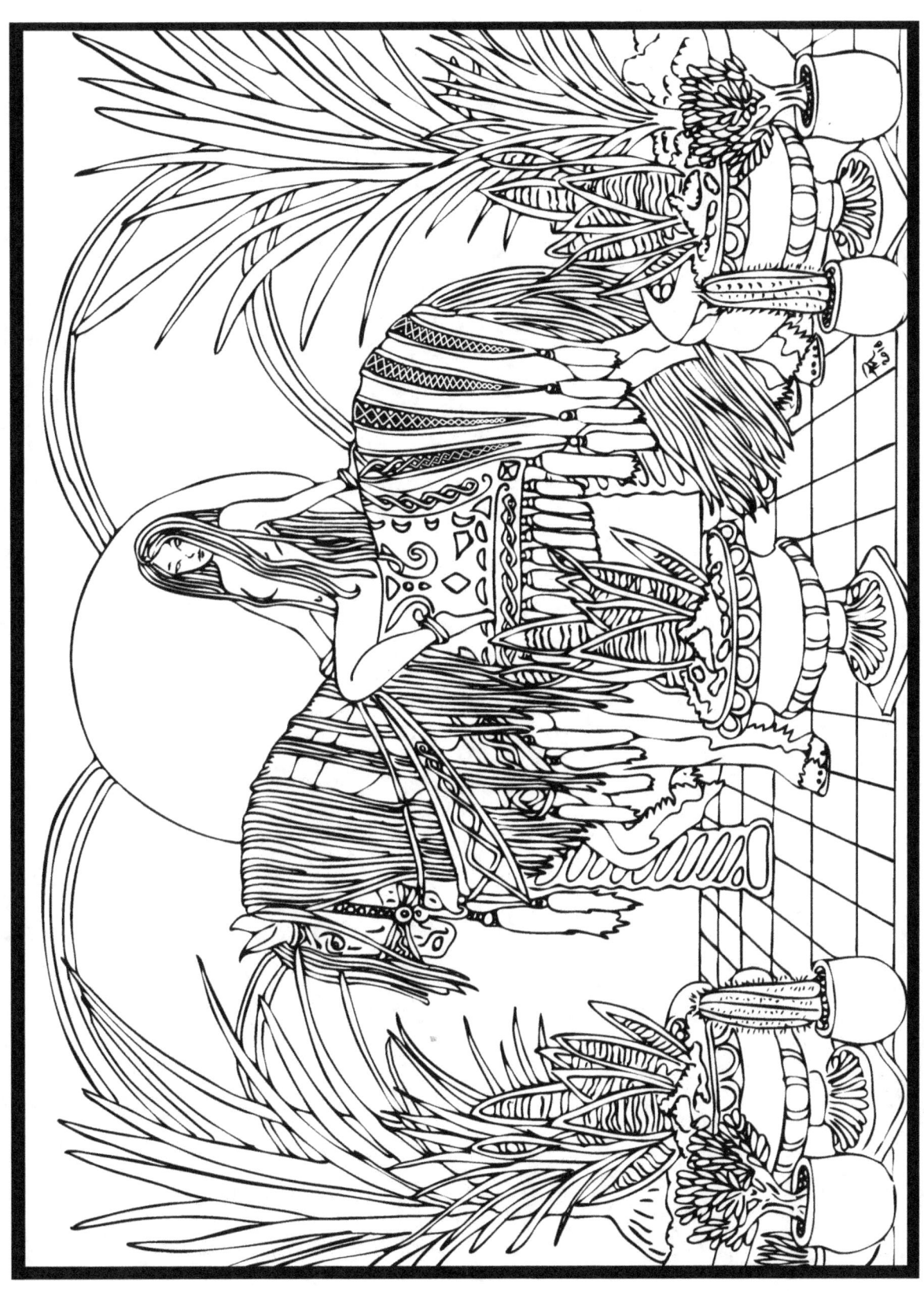

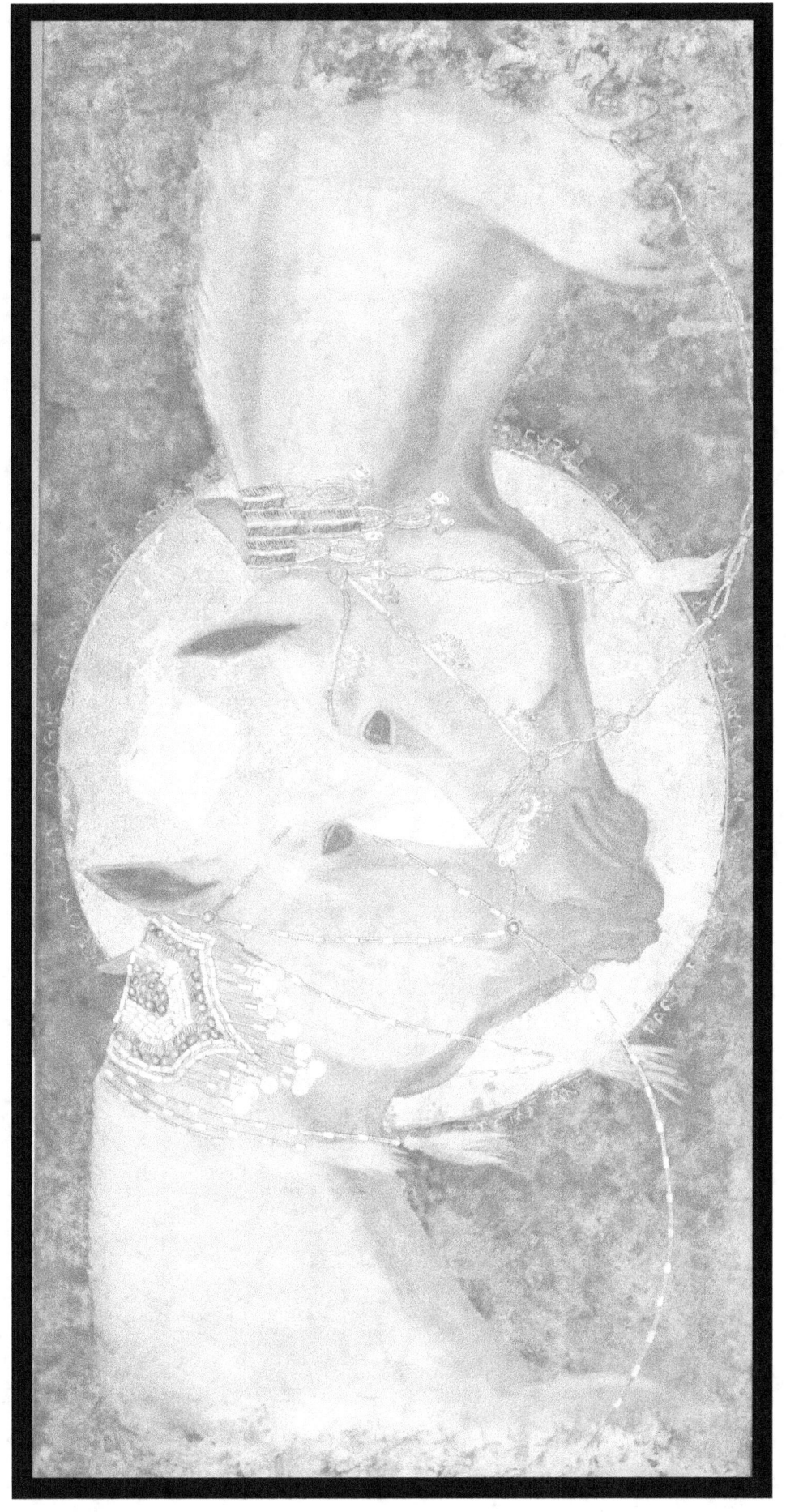

Kathleen Herrington

this is Exclusivo - a horse that changed the course of my life! I travelled to Spain to look for a horse for a friend - my agent,and mentor was also with us, and after my friend had not got on too well with this horse - suggested that I just have a sit on him. It was magic - we just 'clicked'. Although I already had a young Spanish horse - and this fella was older and not in brilliant condition - I had to bring him home -

and he has repaid me a thousand times!

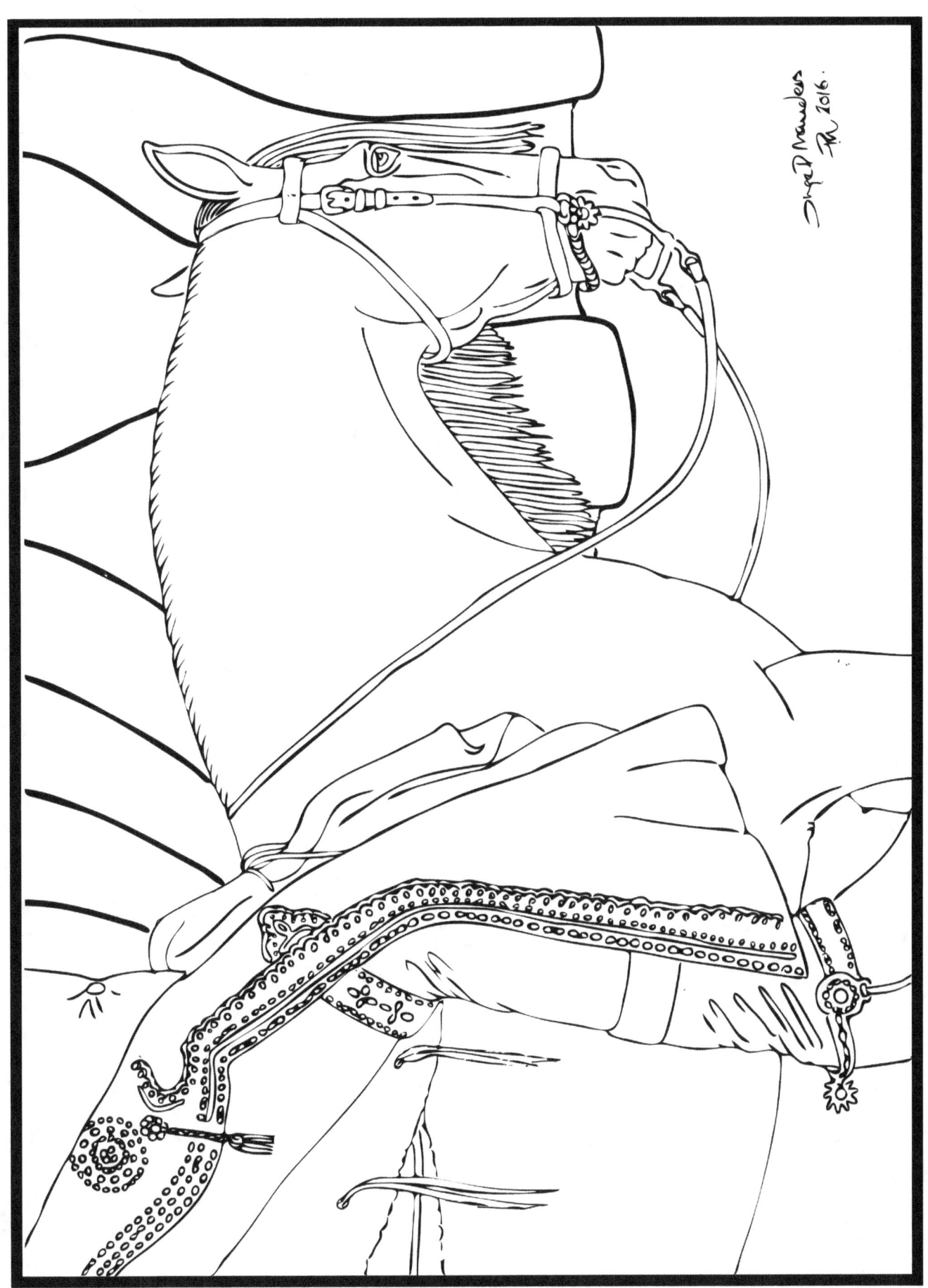

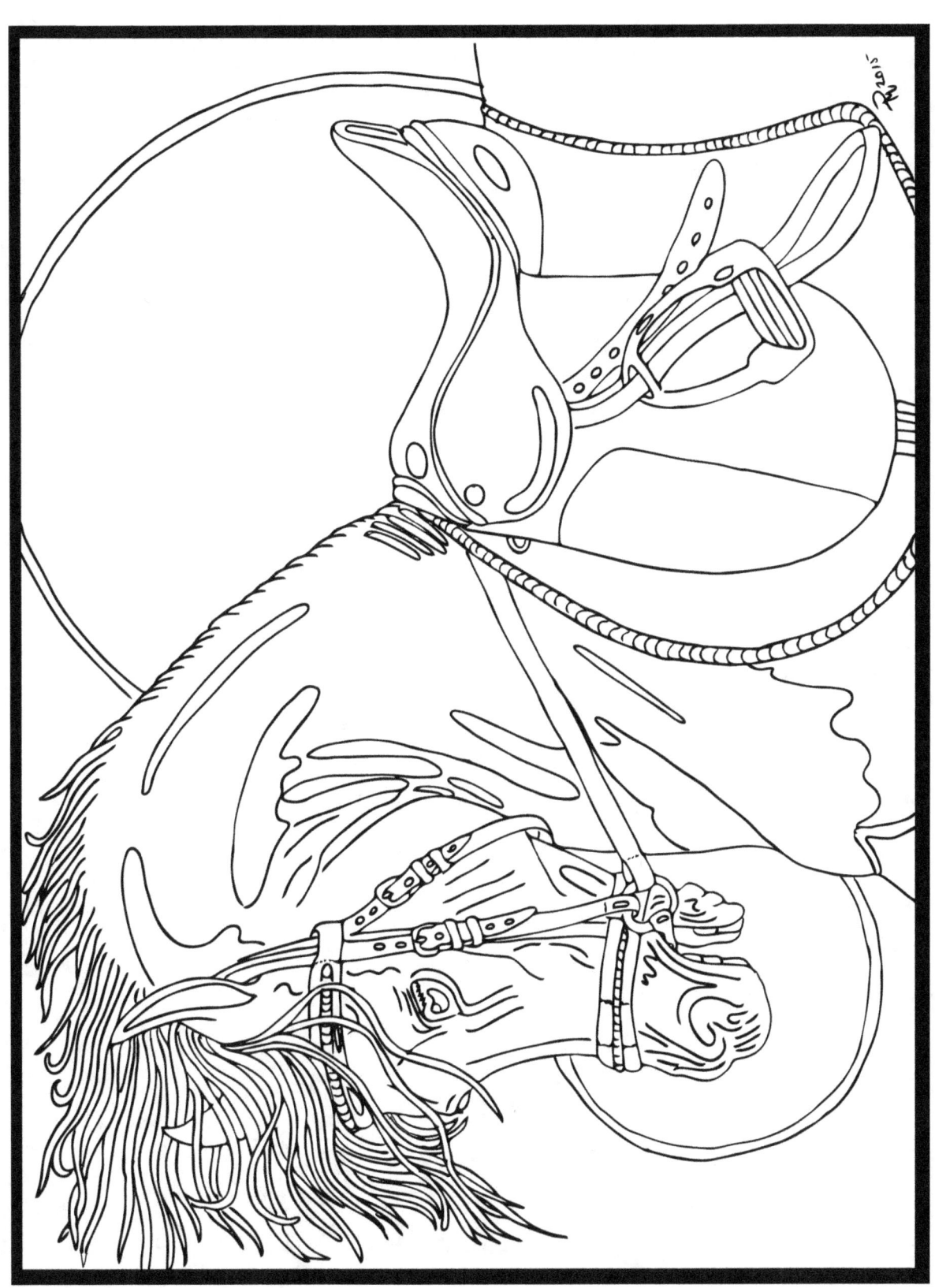

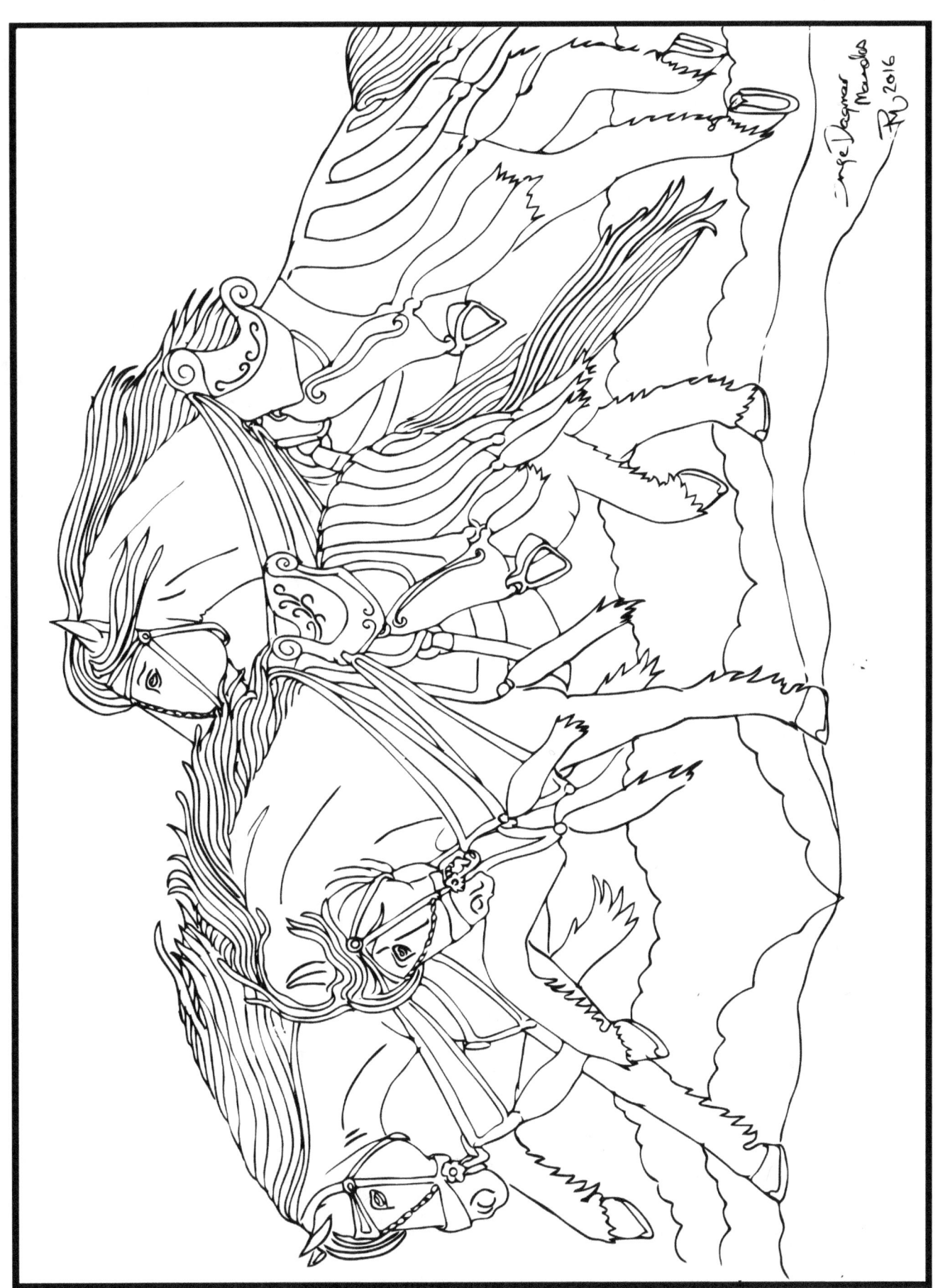

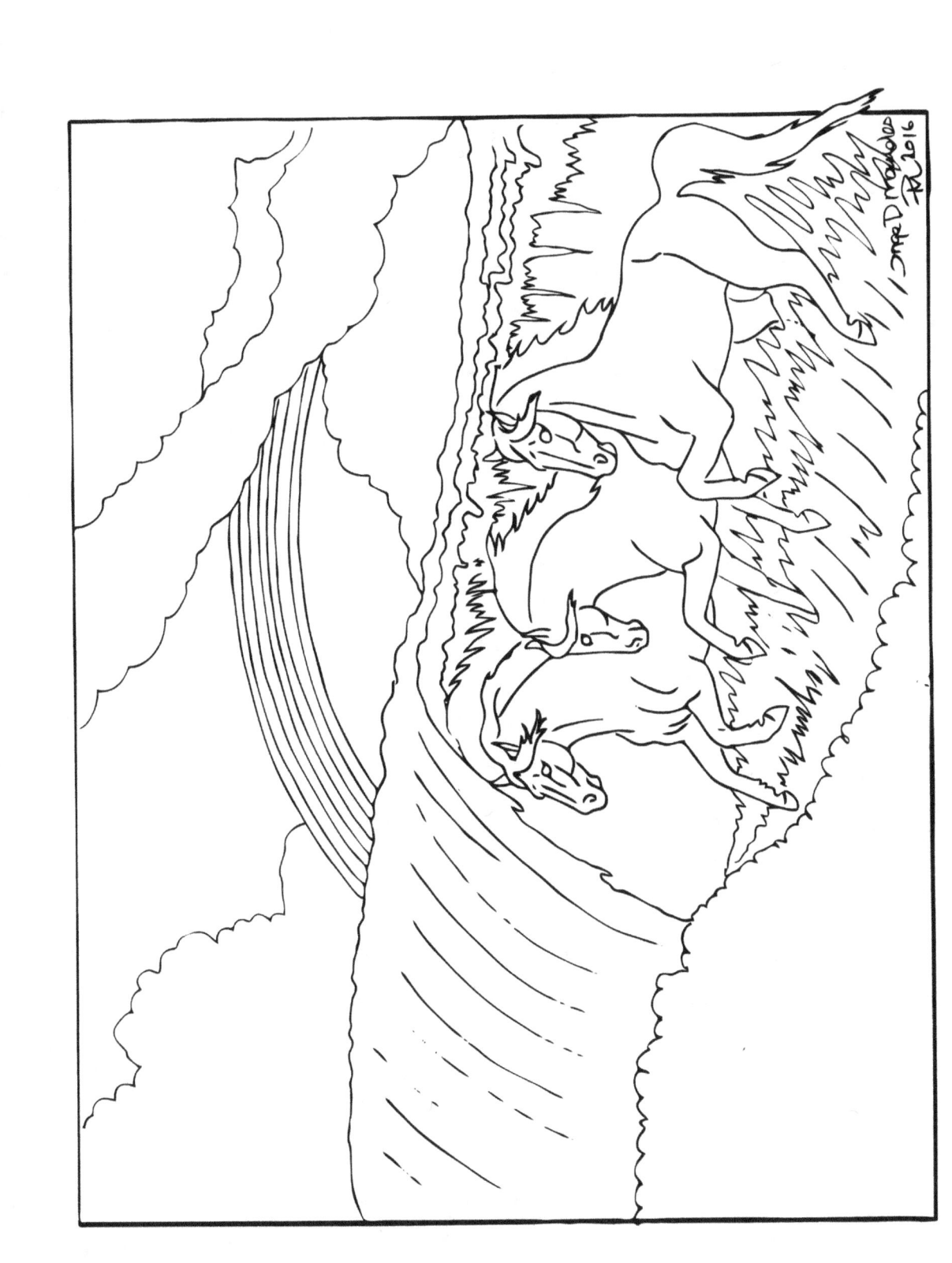

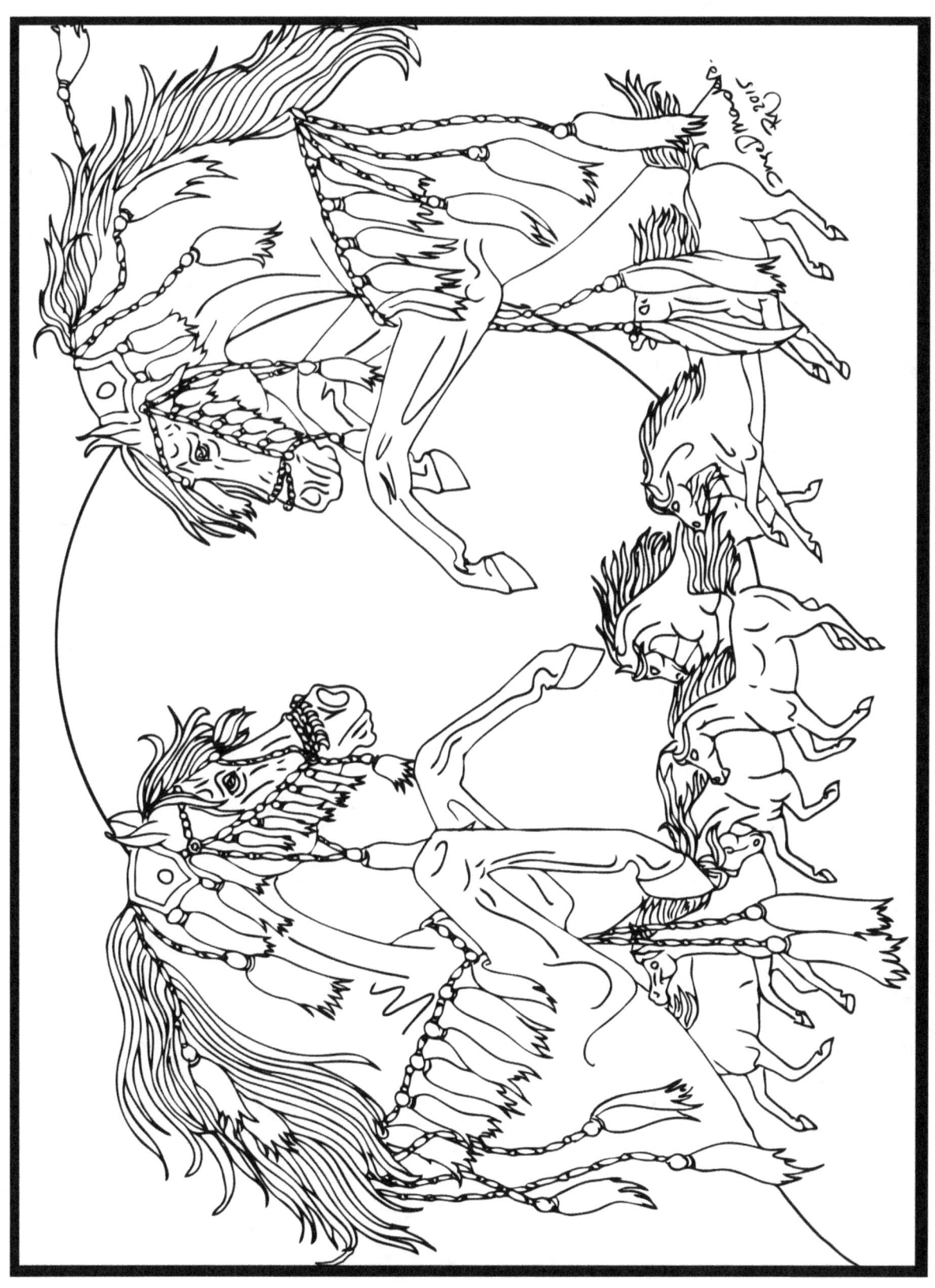

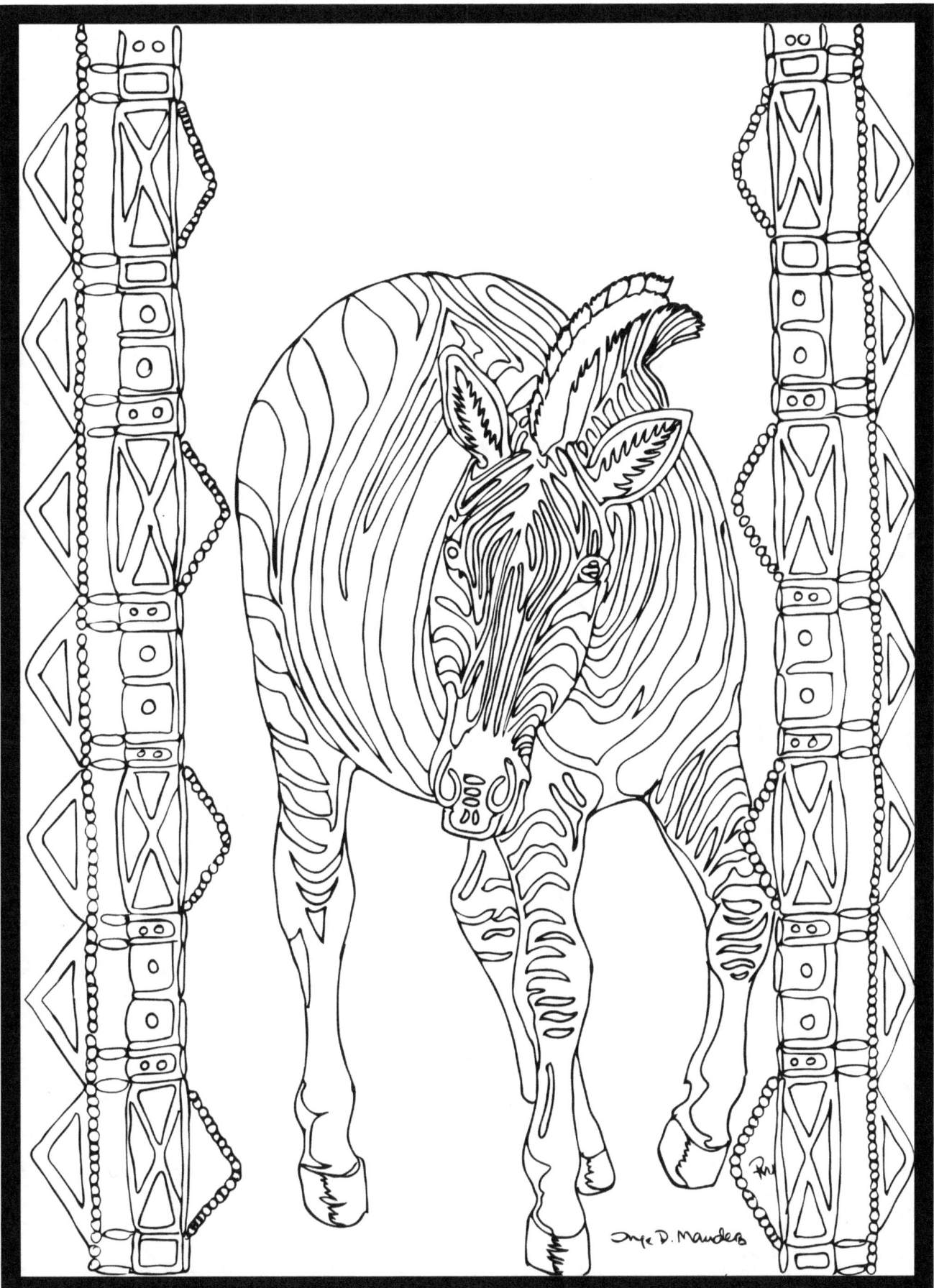

Inge Dagmar Manders.

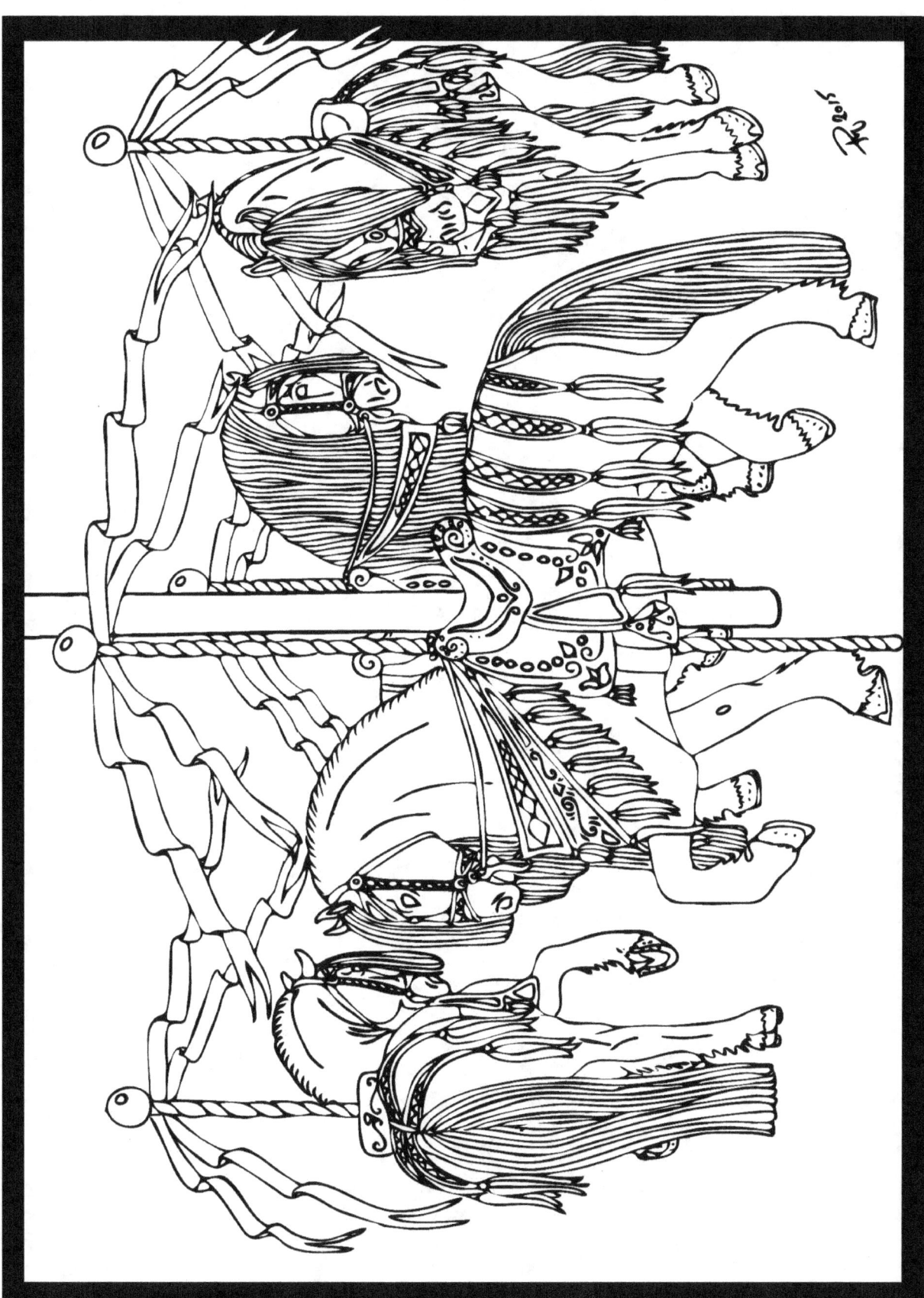

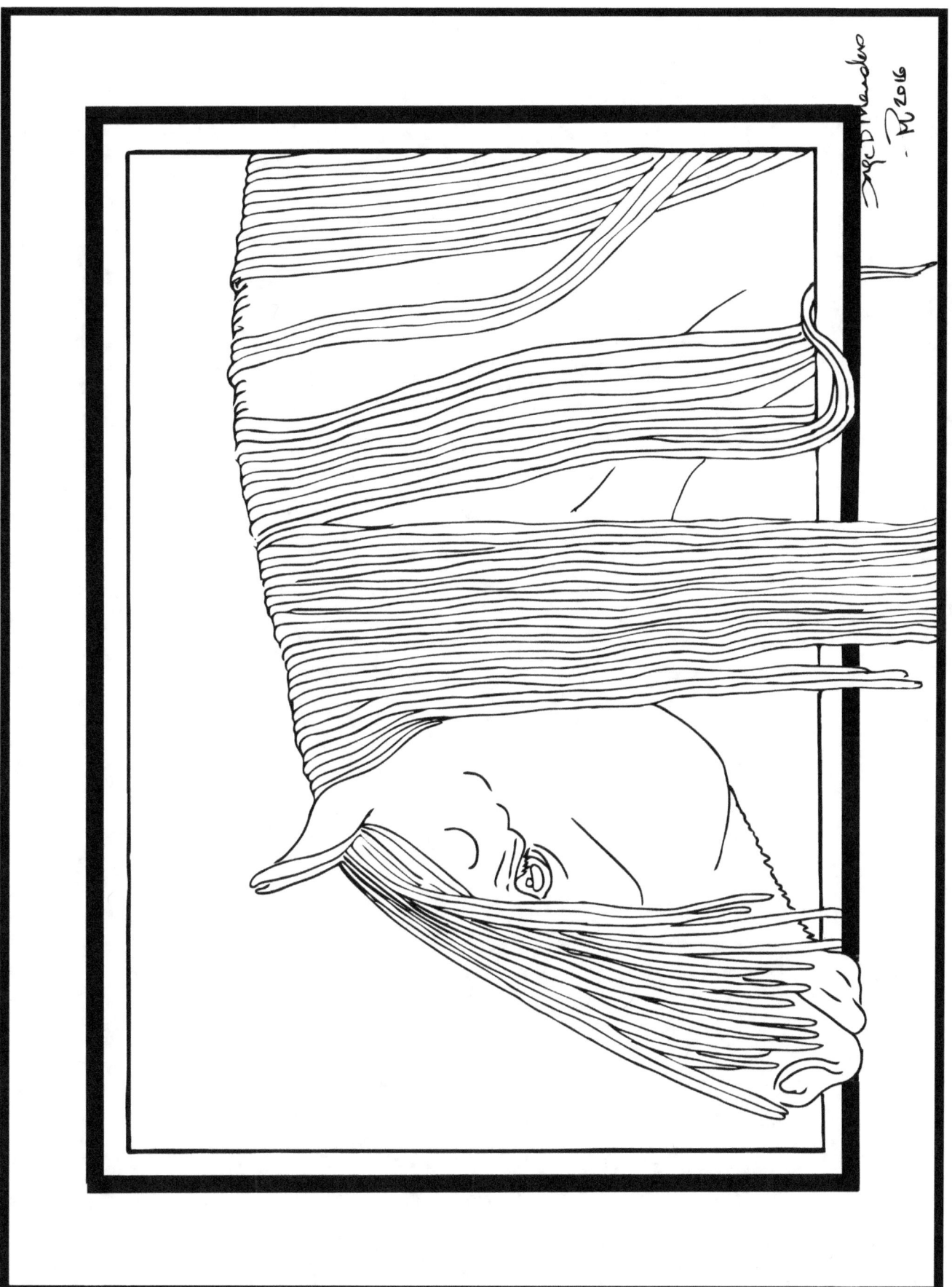

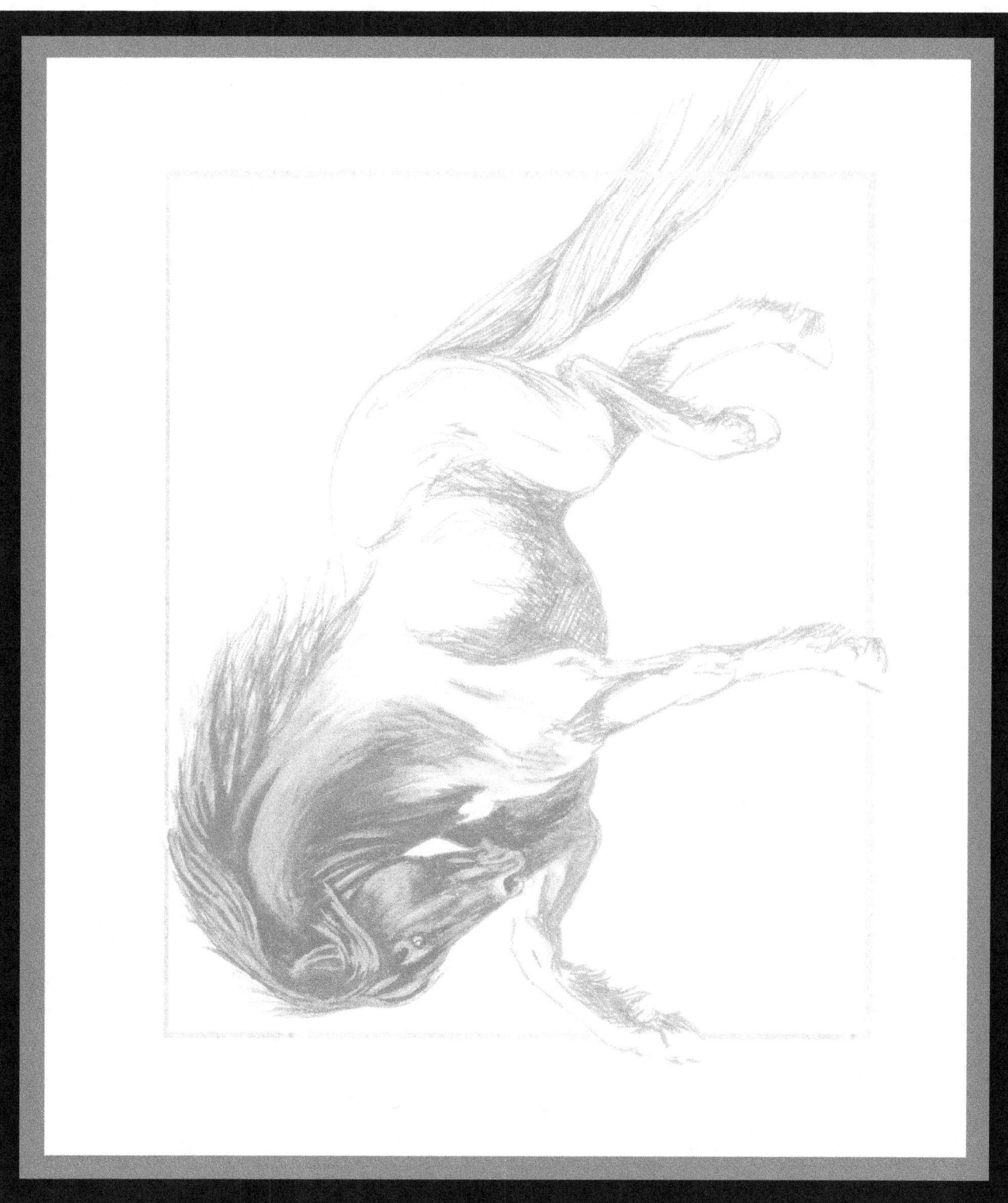

Wynn Amante
Mountain Horses playing

Marie-Justine Roy

Here is Bonanza, the seventh foal of my former mare Friday McLeod, Quarter horse breed. He was born on 28 April and was a cutie, sweet little boy. He had a "7" on his forehead, I miss him and my mare....

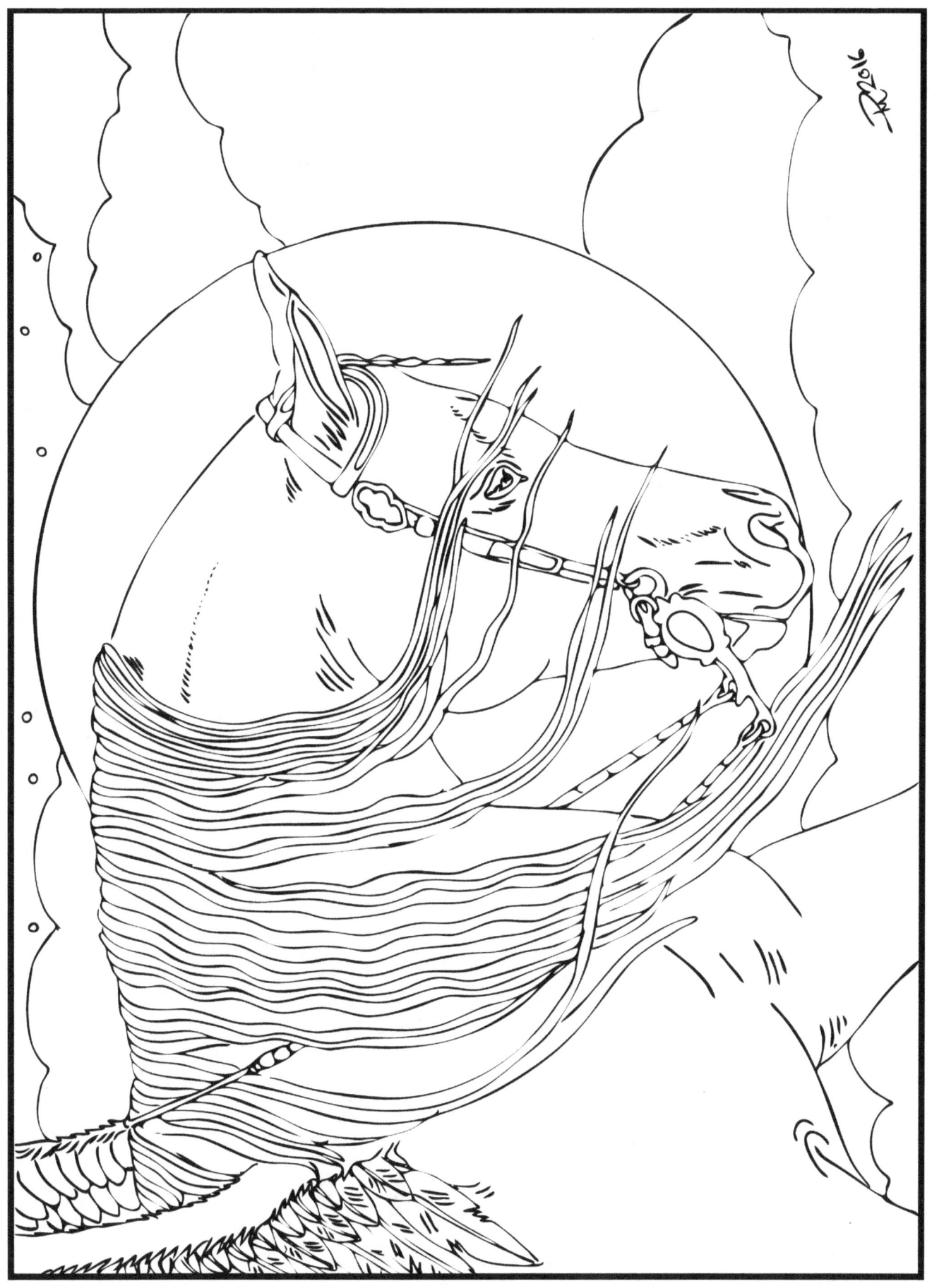

Summer Poupore

Hi. This is HB Rafs Scherazon. She was my first horse. She was 29 when she crossed the rainbow bridge on 5/11/16. A piece of my heart is missing.

Tine Louise Eintzen

My beautiful Graze.

Grazeful Frosted Sazzy ES is my second foal. She is a very special pony.

She was born on April 17th in 2008. She was everything I could ever have wished for and more. As a foal she received premium when she was showed and again as a 2 year old mare she was given a premium title.

She has the best temper I have ever experienced in a young horse and she have brought me so many great experiences. I feel so very lucky to have her and I hope she can be with me till she dies of very old age.

As a 3 year old she was best mare and mare of the day across age. She was invited to the elite mare show in Germany. I almost didn't go. I was so intimidated, because Germany have some of the very best ponies in the world and they are way better quality than in Denmark. But we went - and gosh I'm glad we did. She was announced mare of the year - the best German Riding pony mare also called

Racesiegerin. I still can't believe it!

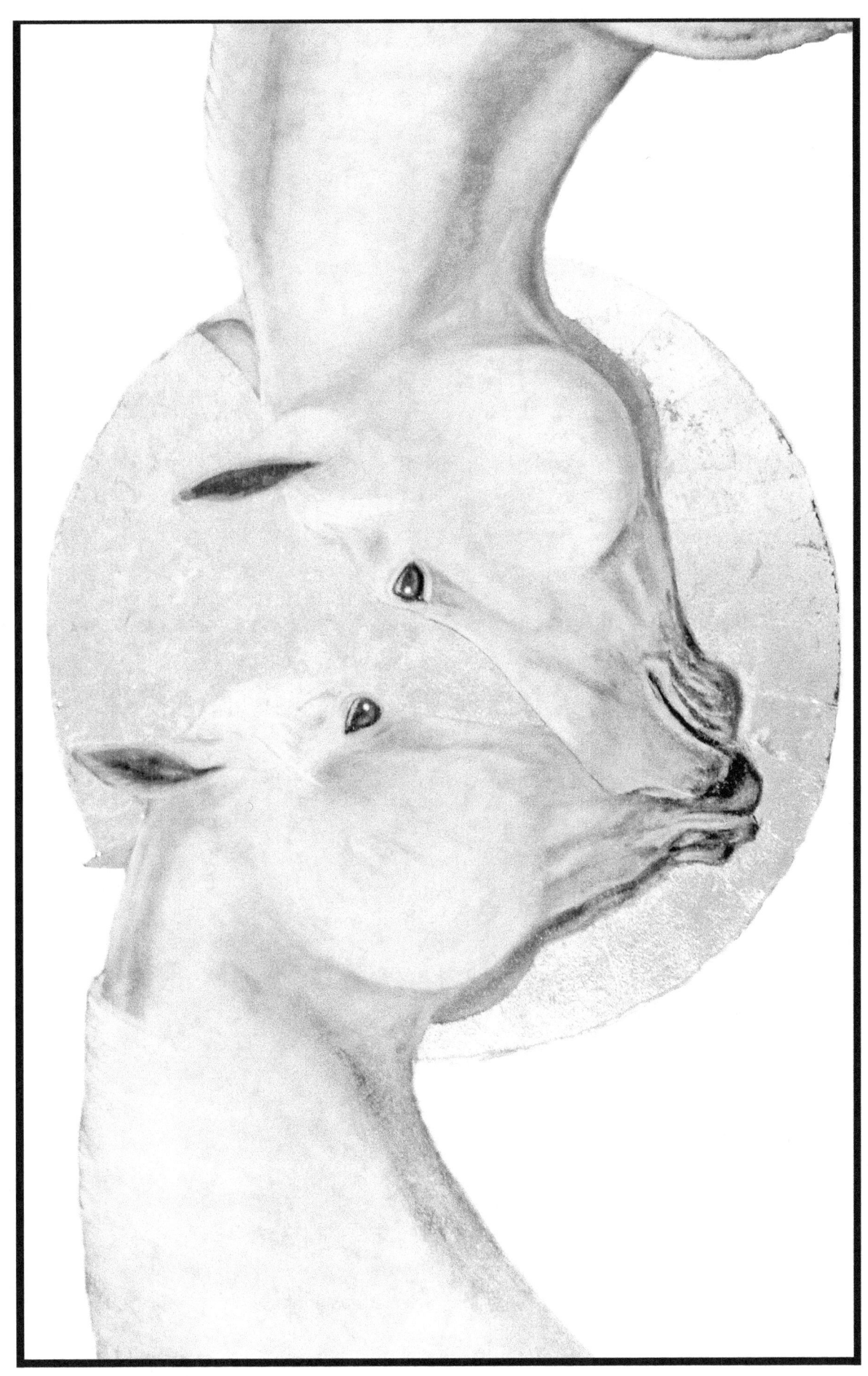

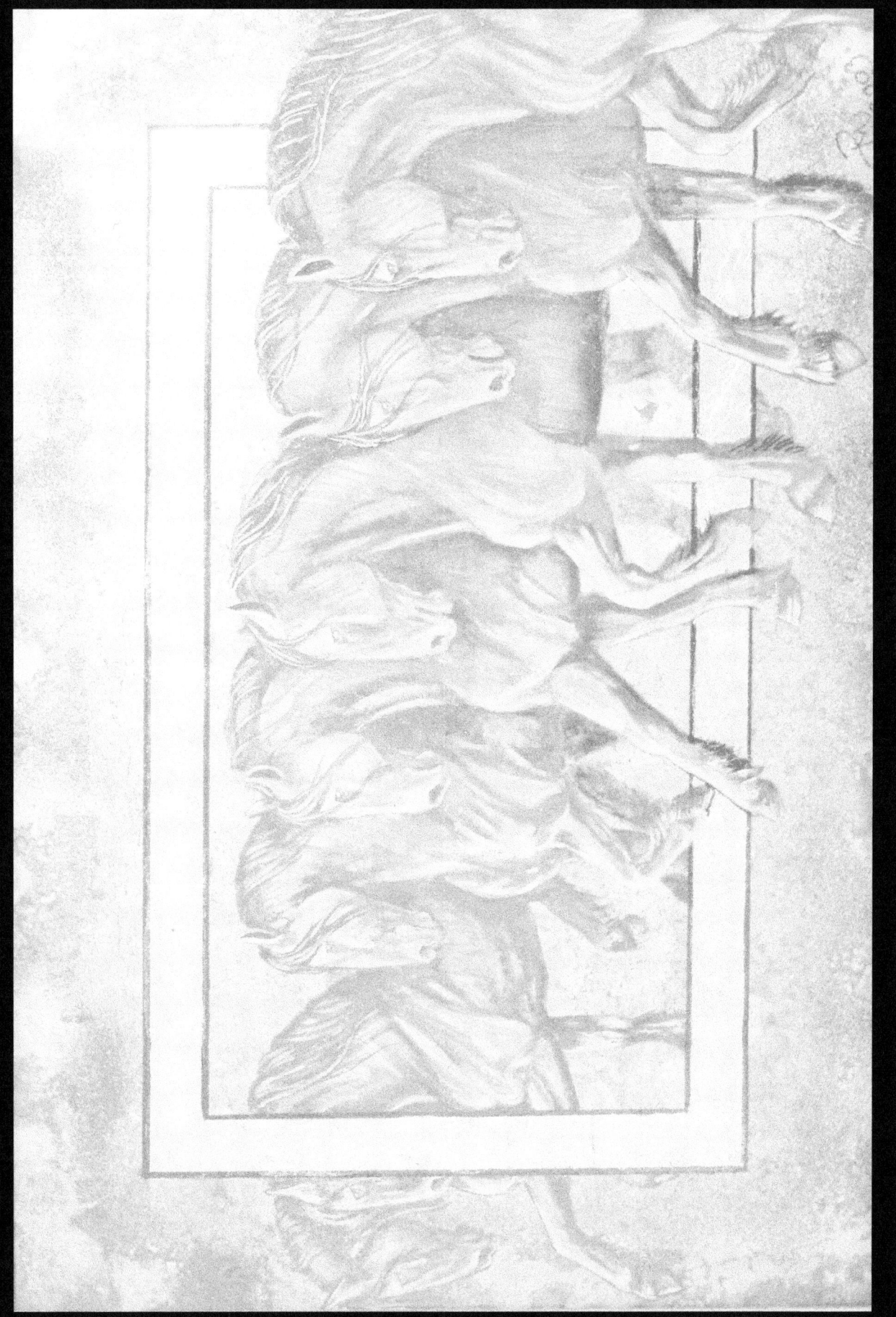

In this next section I thought it would be nice to include some colouring pages for the younger budding artist to enjoy. Introducing Kurt that happy Friesian. Based on the Friesian gelding I used to own. He used to get up to sorts of mischief . With each horse colouring book that I put out your kids can follow his antics...in this book we see him frolicking in the 4 seasons....hope your kids enjoy colouring him :)

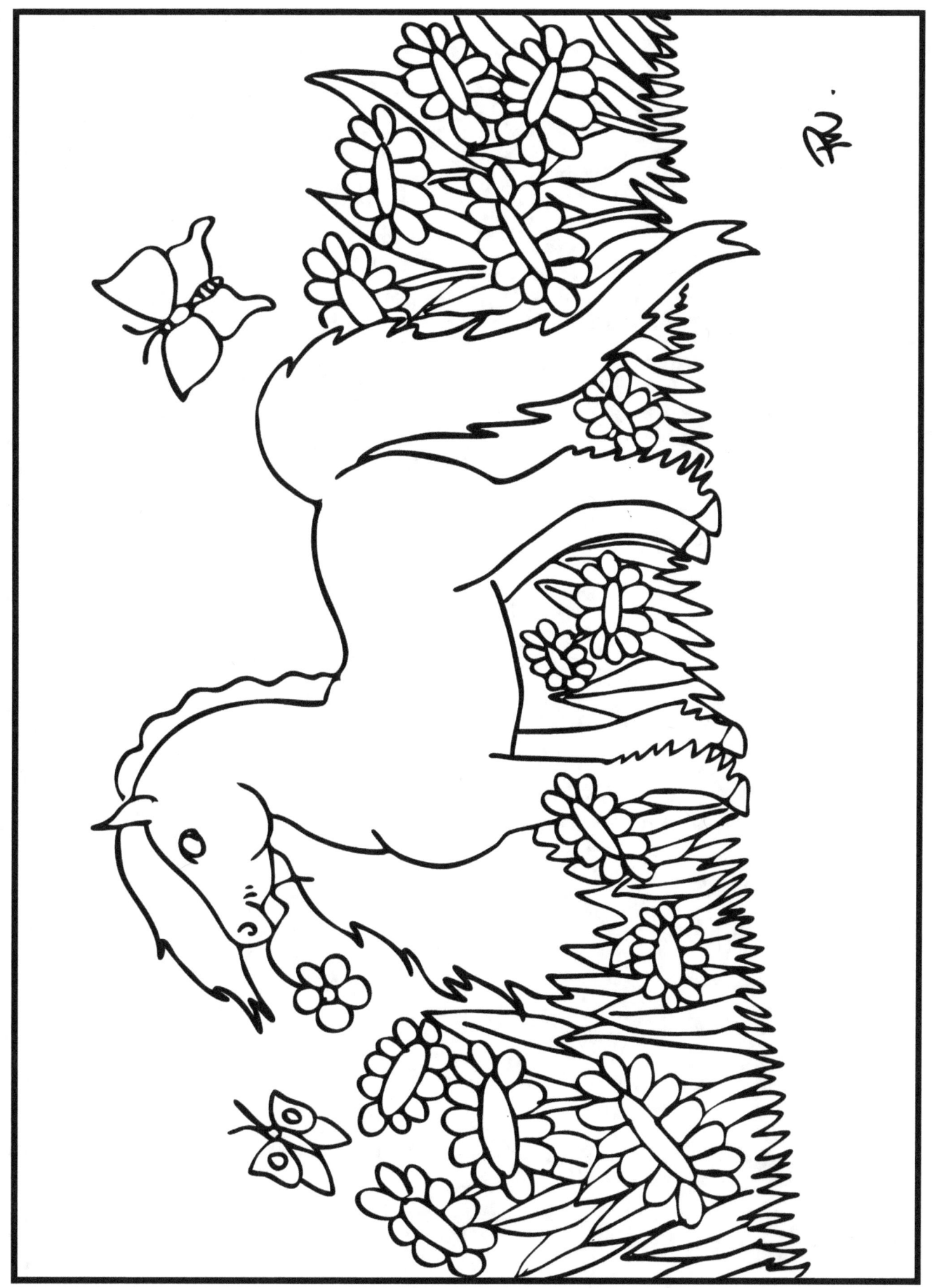

The End

Pencil test page.

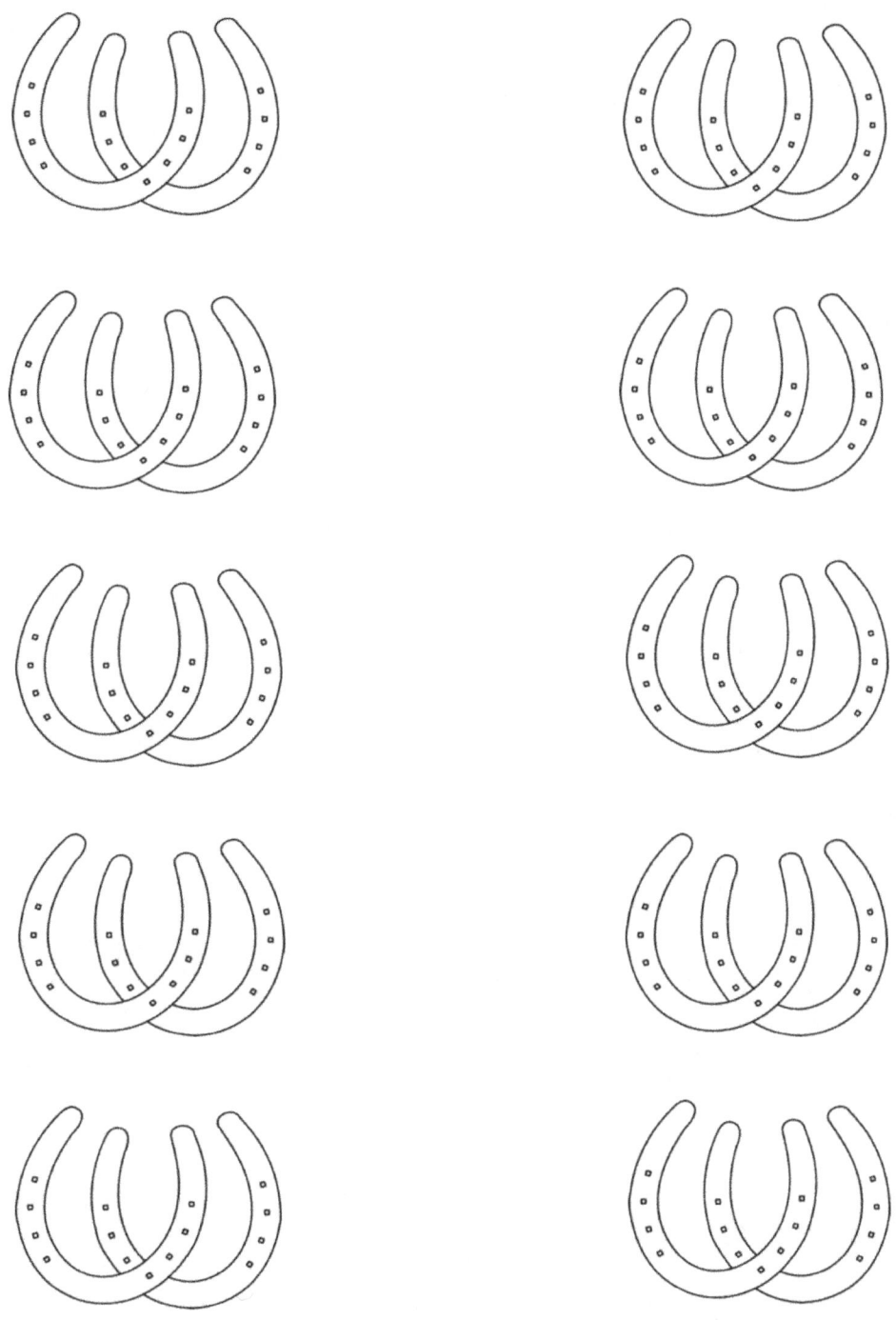

Test page for markers

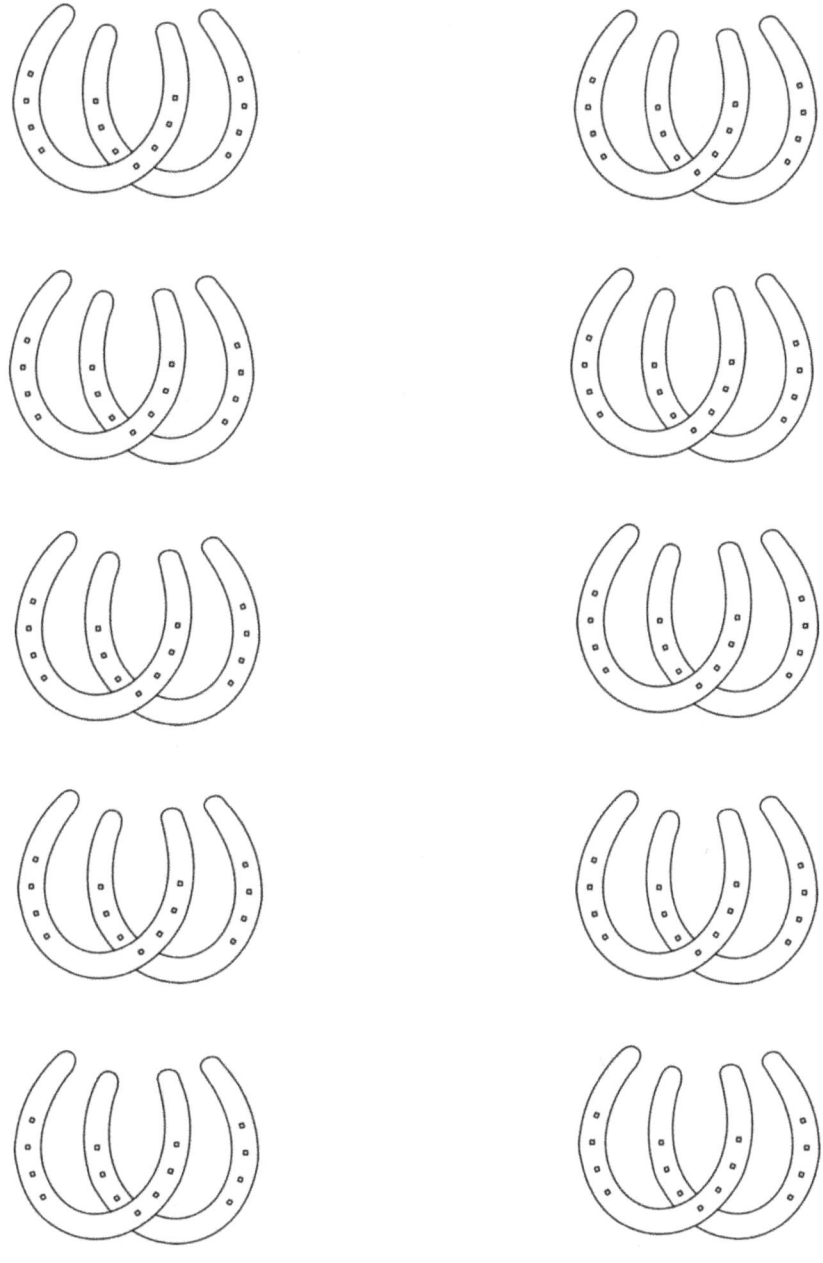

I would like to thank my talented colouring team.
Deb Rucinski
Robin Wilson Nelson
Rebecca Williams
Janice Harbron Matthews
Deidra Acosta
Vero Pignot
Hilda Parro-Lumibao
Marie-Justine Roy
Vickie Hilton
Tine Louise Eintzen
Debbie Wyatt-Lawes
Julie Shirley